KALIDASA

Meghaduta

Also by Abhay K.

Poetry Collections

Enigmatic Love
Fallen Leaves of Autumn
Candling the Light
Remains
The Seduction of Delhi
The Eight-eyed Lord of Kathmandu
The Prophecy of Brasilia
The Alphabets of Latin America

Edited Books

CAPITALS
100 Great Indian Poems
100 More Great Indian Poems
New Brazilian Poems
The Bloomsbury Anthology of Great Indian Poems
The Bloomsbury Book of Great Indian Love Poems
100 Grandes Poemas da Índia
Cien Grandes Poemas de la India
100 Grandi Poesie Indiane
Tononkalo Indianina 100 Tsara Indriandra
100 Grands Poèmes Indiens

Translated Books

Ritusamhara by Kalidasa

Memoirs

River Valley to Silicon Valley
The Colours of Soul

KALIDASA

Meghaduta

THE CLOUD MESSENGER

Translated by
ABHAY K.

BLOOMSBURY
NEW DELHI • LONDON • OXFORD • NEW YORK • SYDNEY

BLOOMSBURY INDIA
Bloomsbury Publishing India Pvt Ltd
Second Floor, LSC Building No. 4, DDA Complex, Pocket C – 6 & 7,
Vasant Kunj, New Delhi 110070

BLOOMSBURY, BLOOMSBURY INDIA and the Diana logo
are trademarks of Bloomsbury Publishing Plc

First published in India 2021
This edition published 2021

Disclaimer: The translator's views and interpretations are his own.

ISBN: PB: 978-93-90252-34-3; e-book: 978-93-90252-36-7

2 4 6 8 10 9 7 5 3 1

Printed and bound in India by Replika Press Pvt Ltd

To find out more about our authors and books, visit
www.bloomsbury.com and sign up for our newsletters

PRAISE FOR THE TRANSLATION OF MEGHADUTA OF KALIDASA BY ABHAY K.

"Very well translated, Abhay K.'s translation of *Meghaduta* gives a fresh sense of the original"

– A.N.D. Haksar

well known translator of Sanskrit works, many published as Penguin Classics

"…work of the highest quality."

– Christopher Merrill

Poet & Director, International Writing Programme, University of Iowa

TRANSLATOR'S NOTE

The Guardian published a poem titled 'Lockdown' by UK poet laureate Simon Armitage on 21st March 2020 about the Corona virus pandemic. It was influenced by *Meghaduta* or *The Cloud Messenger* of Kalidasa. The poem inspired me to read Meghaduta in Sanskrit and its various English translations. I had studied Sanskrit in my high school, which came in handy. My love for it has been growing since then and it has become part of my everyday life.

World Catalogue shows 250 editions of *Meghaduta* so far in various languages. I chose to read the verse translation by H.H. Wilson published over 200 years ago in 1814, prose-poem translation by Col. H.A. Ouvry in 1868, translation with exhaustive notes by Mallinatha published in 1895 and translation by Chandra Rajan published by the Sahitya Akademi in 1997.

These are fine translations. However I felt that this breathtaking poem of 111 stanza needs to be presented to our millennial generation in a more contemporary language. The poem is about a Yaksha or an attendant spirit of Kubera, the Lord of Wealth, who is banished for a year in central India for neglecting his duties in the mythical city of Alaka, in the high Himalayas near Mount Kailasa. He pleads the cloud to be his messenger and take his message to his beloved young wife in Alaka.

Meghaduta is full of detailed descriptions of flora and fauna of the Central and North India as well as of their hills, rivers, mountains, legends, beliefs, traditions, mythologies, rituals, high erotica among others. I have tried my best to preserve the names of the plants and animals, rivers, hills and mountains, traditions and styles, as in the original Sanskrit text of Kalidasa, providing their modern names in the note below each stanza in which they appear. I think it is very important to keep their original names lest we forget them and lose these treasures.

Meghaduta creates a complete magical world in itself full of sylphs, nymphs, spirits, eight-legged animals, the wish fulfilling tree, various kinds of drums, celestial elephants, birds, rare flowers, fruits, plants and trees who help the cloud in his journey to deliver the Yaksha's message to his beloved.

The secret of *Meghaduta's* continued relevance even today, in my view, rests on its focus on sensual love and nature's beauty, the two subjects which are of eternal interest to us; and Kalidasa's genius in making these two flow into each other. For example, who but Kalidasa can imagine the rivers as sensuous women, advising his friend, the cloud to take interest in the rivers along the way on his journey from the central Indian plains to the Himalayas—

तस्या: किंचित्करधृतमिव प्राप्तवानीरशाखं
हृत्वा नीलं सलिलवसनं मुक्तरोधोनितम्बम
प्रस्थानं ते कथम अपि सखे लम्बमानस्य भावि
ज्ञातास्वादो विवृतजघनां को विहातुं समर्थ: || ४१ ||

Like the slender arms of the lady river,
Vanira branches reach out to take away her
water garment and expose her thighs, the banks.
O friend, of course it would take long for you
to depart, for who has the strength to leave
a woman after relishing her bare thighs? 41

This love poem would be unimaginable without all the plants and fragrant flowers described in detail by Kalidasa. This is why *Meghaduta* should be of interest to the contemporary readers as we deal with biodiversity loss and climate change today. Can we use the imagery/idea of nature as a sensual being presented by

Kalidasa in *Meghaduta* to transform how we see nature—from mother to beloved, from revering it to loving it and from being separate from it to being part of it? Can it help us in protecting nature if we start to see clouds, rivers, plants, trees and animals as sensual beings?

Meghaduta also highlights the importance of flowers, plants, animals, seasons, rains, rainbows, winds, sun, moon, stars, stones, rivers, mountains among others things—animate and inanimate, in our love-life, without which we would gradually become bio-robots obsessed with numbers and statistics, dealing with various kinds of growth rates, and living a dismal life on a planet marred by loss of biodiversity and extreme climatic events.

For example—

गत्युत्कम्पादलकपतितैर्यत्रमन्दारपुष्पैः
क्लृप्तच्छेद्यैः कनककमलैः कर्णविभ्रंशिभिश्च।
मुक्तालग्नस्तनपरिमलैश्छिन्नसूत्रैश्च हारैर्
नैशो मार्गः सवितुरुदये सूच्यते कामिनीनाम् || ६७ ||

Where at dawn, the night-path of the amorous women
are revealed by fallen Mandara flowers from their ringlets,
golden lotuses torn, fallen from their ears,
threads of their necklaces broken, pearls scattered,
fragrant from the perfume of their breasts. 67

I hope my translation of *Meghaduta* in contemporary English but staying true to the letter and spirit of Kalidasa's Sanskrit original, gives you a taste of undiminished beauty and splendour of this classic poem written circa 5th century CE. I have also provided the original Sanskrit text.

Lockdown across the planet has taught us to pay attention to our surroundings as Kalidasa has done in this exquisite poem, reminding us of all the beauty waiting to be discovered by slowing down, listening to birdsong, smelling the fragrance of flowers, reading books, thinking about our relationship with the nature and how to tackle the three biggest challenges our planet faces today—biodiversity loss, climate change and environmental pollution.

Bon Voyage with the Cloud!

– Abhay K.

कश्चित्कान्ताविरहगुरुणा स्वाधिकारात्प्रमत्तः
शापेनास्तंगमितमहिमा वर्षभोग्येण भर्तुः
यक्षश्चक्रे जनकतनयास्नानपुण्योदकेषु
स्निग्धच्छायातरुषु वसतिं रामगिर्याश्रमेषु ॥१॥

A Yaksha, negligent of his duties,
deprived of his divinity by Kubera's curse,
banished for a year away from his beloved,
made home at hermitages in Ramagiri
full of thick and shady groves
where Sita bathed once. 1

Yaksha: attendant spirit of Kubera, the god of wealth in Hindu mythology

तस्मिन्नद्रौ कतिचिदबलाविप्रयुक्तः स कामी
नीत्वा मासान् कनकवलयभ्रंशरिक्तप्रकोष्ठः
आषाढस्य प्रथमदिवसे मेघमाश्लिष्टसानुं
वप्रक्रीडापरिणतगजप्रेक्षणीयं ददर्श ॥२॥

Separated from his sweetheart—lovesick,
having passed several months on these hills
his arms bare—golden bracelets fallen off,
on the first day of Asadha, he saw a cloud
embracing the mountain peak, like an elephant
engaged in playful thrusts against a river bank. 2

Asadha: the first month of the rainy season, usually in June-July

तस्य स्थित्वा कथमपि पुरः कौतुकाधानहेतो
रन्तर्बाष्पश्चिरमनुचरो राजराजस्य दध्यौ
मेघालोके भवति सुखिनोऽप्यन्यथावृत्ति चेतः
कण्ठाश्लेषप्रणयिनि जने किं पुनर्दूरसंस्थे ॥३॥

Standing before it with tearful eyes
he fell into deep trance—even a happy
heart is moved at the sight of a cloud,
what then could be the state of someone
who has been exiled so far away—
full of desire, anxious to embrace his love? 3

प्रत्यासन्ने नभसि दयिताजीवितालम्बनार्थी
जीमूतेन स्वकुशलमयीं हारयिष्यन्प्रवृत्तिम
स प्रत्यग्रैः कुटजकुसुमैः कल्पितार्घाय तस्मै
प्रीतः प्रीतिप्रमुखवचनं स्वागतं व्याजहार ॥४॥

Nabhasa setting in, he craved to please his love,
sending her a word through the cloud
so he made an offering of fresh Kutaja flowers
to the cloud and addressed him dearly. 4

Nabhasa: the second month of rainy season in India usually in July/ August

Kutaja: Ivory tree (Holarrhena antidysenterica)

धूमज्योतिःसलिलमरुतां संनिपातः क्व मेघः
सन्देशार्थाः क्व पटुकरणैः प्राणिभिः प्रापणीयाः
इत्यौत्सुक्यादपरिगणयन् गुह्यकस्तं ययाचे
कामार्ता हि प्रकृतिकृपणाश्चेतनाचेतएषु ॥५॥

Can a cloud, a concoction of water and wind,
radiant vapour and lightning carry a message,
usually done by a wise messenger in flesh and bone?
He urged the cloud without paying attention
to these, mad in love—for the lovesick
what's animate and what's inanimate? 5

जातं वंशे भुवनविदिते पुष्करावर्तकानां
जानामि त्वां प्रकृतिपुरुषं कामरूपं मघोन:
तेनार्थित्वं त्वयि विधिवशाद् दूरबन्धुर्गतोऽहं
याच्ञा मोघा वरमधिगुणे नाधमे लब्धकामा: ॥६॥

The lineage of legendary Pushakaravartas—
the shape-shifters at will, the Prime Minister of Indra,
separated from my love by fate, I pray to you—
for seeking favours from the deft, even if denied,
is better than a wish granted by the inept. 6

Pushkaravartas: water bearing clouds

संतप्तानां त्वमसि शरणं तत्पयोद प्रियायाः
संदेशं मे हर धनपतिक्रोधविश्लेषितस्य
गन्तव्या ते वसतिरलका नाम यक्षेश्वराणां
बाह्योद्यानस्थितहरशिरश्चन्द्रिकाधौतहर्म्या ||७||

O rainmaker, the saviour of the suffering,
please carry my message to my true love—
for I am separated from her by the wrath of Kubera,
please go to Alaka, the residence of the Lord of Yaksha,
where palaces glow under the moon on Shiva's head,
who resides in the gardens on the city's outskirts. 7

त्वामारूढं पवनपदवीमुद्गृहीतालकान्ताः
प्रेक्षिष्यन्ते पथिकवनिताः प्रत्ययादाश्वसन्त्यः।
कः संनद्धे विरहविधुरां त्वय्युपेक्षेत जायां
न स्यादन्योऽप्यहमिव जनो यः पराधीनवृत्तिः। ॥८॥

The travellers' wives confident
that their husbands would return soon
with their Veni uplifted, will look at you
advancing with the wind. Who would
neglect his wife distressed by separation,
when you are near, at hand? 8

Veni: top-knot of hair tied by Indian women in the olden days when their husbands went on journey

मन्दं मन्दं नुदति पवनश चानुकूलो यथा त्वां
वामश चायं नदति मधुरं चातकस ते सगन्धः
गर्भाधानक्षणपरिचयान नूनम आबद्धमालाः
सेविष्यन्ते नयनसुभगं खे भवन्तं बलाकाः ॥९॥

Auspicious wind will push you gently
on your left, thirsty Chataka will sing sweetly,
the Valakas forming a queue will admire you
knowing your arrival is the joyous time of mating
as you float in the sky pleasing their eyes. 9

Chataka: pied crested cuckoo

Valakas: here refer to cranes as well as pretty coquettish bright-eyed women

त्वां चावश्यं दिवसगणनातत्पराम एकपत्नीम
अव्यापन्नाम अविहतगतिर द्रक्ष्यसि भ्रातृजायाम
आशाबन्धः कुसुमसदृशं प्रायशो ह्य अङ्‌गनानां
सद्यः पाति प्रणयि हृदयं विप्रयोगे रुणद्धि ||१०||

On your onward journey, you would
surely see my wife—still alive,
busy counting days. Hope sustains
tender hearts of women, which wilt
readily like a flower after separation. 10

कर्तुं यच च प्रभवति महीम उच्चिलीन्ध्राम अवन्ध्यां
तच च्रुत्वा ते श्रवणसुभगं गर्जितं मानसोत्का:
आ कैलासाद बिसकिसलयच्च्वेदपाथेयवन्त:
संपत्स्यन्ते नभसि भवतो राजहंसा: सहाया: ॥११॥

The Rajhansas, hearing your melodic thunder,
which makes mushrooms grow all over the earth,
longing to go to the Manasa lake will accompany you
in the sky up to mount Kailasa as soon as they make
provisions of fresh lotus stalks for their journey. 11

Rajhansas: the royal swans
Lake Manasa and Mount Kailasa are in the high Himalayas

आपृच्चस्व प्रियसखम अमुं तुङ्गम आलिङ्ग्य शैलं
वन्द्यैः पुंसां रघुपतिपदैर अङ्कितं मेखलासु
काले काले भवति भवतो यस्य संयोगम एत्य
स्नेहव्यक्तिश चिरविरहजं मुञ्चतो बाष्पमुष्णम ॥१२॥

Depart after embracing the lofty peak carrying
footprints of Lord Rama, venerated by the people,
which you visit from season to season showing devotion
—shedding tears caused by extended separation. 12

मर्गं तावच चृणु कथयतस त्वत्प्रयाणानुरूपं
संदेशं मे तदनु जलद श्रोष्यसि श्रोत्रपेयम
खिन्नः खिन्नः शिहरिषु पदं न्यस्य गन्तासि यत्र
क्षीणः क्षीणः परिलघु पयः स्रोतसां चोपभुज्य ॥१३॥

O rain-maker, listen to me
while I tell you the optimal path of your journey,
whenever you're tired you can rest on a mountain,
and when thirsty, drink from a river to refresh yourself,
now lend me your ears for the message to my love. 13

अद्रेः शृङ्गं हरति पवनः किं स्विद इत्य उन्मुखीभिर
दृष्टोत्साहश चकितचकितं मुग्धसिद्धाङ्गनाभिः
स्थानाद अस्मात सरसनिचुलाद उत्पतोदङ्मुखः खं
दिङ्नागानां पथि परिहरन स्थूलहस्तावलेपान ||१४||

While the innocent Siddha virgins looking at the sky,
tremble and crat, fearing the wind would carry off the peak,
fly away from this place full of sap-filled Nicula thickets,
your face turned towards the north, humbling the pride
of strong trunked elephants—the guardians of the sky. 14

Siddhas: inhabitants of the air, Sylphs

Nicula: Salix caprea or Brringtonia acutangula

Elephants are believed, as per the legend, to support and guard the eight-cardinal points of the sky.

रत्नच्चायाव्यतिकर इव प्रेक्ष्यमेतत्पुरस्ताद
वल्मीकाग्रात प्रभवति धनु:खण्डम आखण्डलस्य
येन श्यामं वपुर अतितरां कान्तिम आपत्स्यते ते
बर्हेणेव स्फुरितरुचिना गोपवेषस्य विष्णो: ||१५||

A piece of rainbow will appear in the east
at the top of the Valmika mountain, like blending
of light in the jewels, bestowing your dark blue body
celestial beauty like Vishnu dressed as Krishna
wearing peacock feather with bright colours. 15

त्वय्य आयन्तं कृषिफलम इति भ्रूविकारान अभिज्ञैः
प्रीतिस्निग्धैर्जनपदवधूलोचनैः पीयमानः
सद्यःसीरोत्कषणसुरभि क्षेत्रम आरुह्य मालं
किंचित पश्चाद व्रज लघुगतिर भूय एवोत्तरेण ||१६||

Village maidens will eagerly look at you
unskilled in the amorous eyebrow play
moist with affection, longing for love
knowing fertility of the soil depends on you,
ascend when you reach the fields of Mala
fragrant with fresh ploughing, go a bit westward
gently and then northward with a quick pace. 16

त्वाम आसारप्रशमितवनोपप्लवं साधु मूर्ध्ना
वक्ष्यत्य अध्वश्रमपरिगतं सानुमान आम्रकूटः
न क्षुद्रोऽपि प्रथमसुकृतापेक्षया संश्रयाय
प्राप्ते मित्रे भवति विमुखः किं पुनर यस तथोच्चैः ॥१७॥

O extinguisher of forest fires with your heavy showers,
Mountain Amrakuta will crown you on its peak,
tired as you'll be, even a vile doesn't turn away one's face
from a friend seeking shelter, aware of his past favours,
what to speak of someone so lofty! 17

चन्नोपान्तः परिणतफलद्योतिभिः काननाम्रैस
त्वय्य आरूढे शिखरम अचलः स्निग्धवेणीसवर्णे
नूनं यास्यत्य अमरमिथुनप्रेक्षणीयाम अवस्थां
मध्ये श्यामः स्तन इव भुवः शेषविस्तारपाण्डुः ॥१८॥

The mountain slopes shaded with shining ripe fruits
of wild Amras, you will resemble a shiny curl
climbing its peak, worthy of a glance of the celestial
couple—you dark in the middle, like Earth's nipple,
amidst the light-golden in the remaining expanse. 18

Amras: Mangoes

स्थित्वा तस्मिन वनचरवधूभुक्तकुञ्जे मुहूर्तं
तोयोत्सर्गद्रुततरगतिस तत्परं वर्त्म तीर्णः
रेवां द्रक्ष्यस्य उपलविषमे विन्ध्यपादे विशीर्णां
भक्तिच्चेदैर इव विरचितां भूतिम अङ्गे गजस्य ॥१९॥

Having rested for a while in its shades
enjoyed by the forest dwellers' wives,
becoming lighter by discharging water,
traversing the path beyond the mountain,
you'll see the Reva parted into many rivulets
at the rugged foot of the Vindhyas
like an elephant decorated with coloured stripes. 19

Reva: Narmada river
Vindhyas: a mountain range in the west-central India

तस्यास तिक्तैर वनगजमदैर वासितं वान्तवृष्टिर
जम्बूकुञ्जप्रतिहतरयं तोयम आदाय गच्चे:
अन्त:सारं घन तुलयितुं नानिल: शक्ष्यति त्वां
रिक्त: सर्वो भवति हि लघु: पूर्णता गौरवाय ||२०||

The river fragrant with secretions of wild elephants
in their mating season, her streams obstructed
by Jambu bushes, you, exhausted from pouring out rain,
should drink water here before proceeding. Drunk on water,
O dark and handsome one, the wind would not take you lightly,
for emptiness makes things light, fullness confers weight. 20

Jambu: Java plum (Syzygium cumini)

नीपं दृष्ट्वा हरितकपिशं केसरैर अर्धरूढैर
आविर्भूतप्रथममुकुलाः कन्दलीश चानुकच्चम
जग्ध्वारण्येष्व अधिकसुरभिं गन्धम आघ्राय चोर्व्याः
सारङ्गास ते जललवमुचः सूचयिष्यन्ति मार्गम ॥२१॥

Having seen the Nipa flowers appear greenish red
with half grown stamens, the first buds of the Kandalis
emerge along the bank, savouring the fragrance
of earth in the burnt woods, antelopes will guide you,
O sprinkler of water! 21

Kandali: a stout herbaceous plant, Elephant Foot Yam

उत्पश्यामि द्रुतमपि सखे मत्प्रियार्थं यियासोः
कालक्षेपं ककुभसुरभौ पर्वते पर्वते ते
शुक्लापाङ्गैः सजलनयनैः स्वागतीकृत्य केकाः
प्रत्युद्यातः कथम अपि भवान गन्तुम आशु व्यवस्येत ॥२२॥

O friend, I foresee, though you would like
to go quickly to my love, the sweet scent of Kakubha
will steal your heart at every mountain,
and the peacocks will welcome you crying
with white corners of their eyes filled with tears of joy.
Wouldn't you somehow advance hastily for me? 22

Kakubha: a large, evergreen tree with fragrant flowers

पाण्डुच्छायोपवनवृतयः केतकैः सूचिभिन्नैर
नीडारम्भैर गृहबलिभुजाम आकुलग्रामचैत्याः
त्वय्य आसन्ने परिणतफलश्यामजम्बूवनान्ताः
संपत्स्यन्ते कतिपयदिनस्थायिहंसा दशार्णाः ॥२३॥

The country of Dasharna will celebrate your arrival,
the garden hedges will become white with Ketaka buds
split open like needles. Joyous, the birds will start
building nests on sacred village trees. The Jambu
forest at its border will darken with its ripe fruits
and the Hamsas will stay for a few more days. 23

Dasharna: Valley of the river Dasan

Ketaka: Pandanus odoratissimus, Screw Pine, white fragrant flowers favourite of gods

Jambu: Java plum

Hamsas: Swans

तेषां दिक्षु प्रथितविदिशालक्षणां राजधानीं
गत्वा सद्यः फलम अविकलं कामुकत्वस्य लब्धा
तीरोपान्तस्तनितसुभगं पास्यसि स्वादु यस्मात
सभ्रूभङ्गं मुखम इव पयो वेत्रवत्याश चलोर्मि ||२४||

When you arrive in Vidisha, the royal city,
the well-known capital in all directions,
you'll at once get pure pleasure as a skilled lover
for you'll drink Vaitrawati's sweet waters
like a lover drinks from his dearest's lips,
as she flows with frowning, unsteady currents
making murmuring sound near the shore. 24

Vaitrawati: Betwa river

नीचौराख्यं गिरिम अधिवसेस तत्र विश्रामहेतोस
त्वत्सम्पर्कात पुलकितम इव प्रौढपुष्पैः कदम्बैः
यः पुण्यस्त्रीरतिपरिमलोद्गारिभिर नागराणाम
उद्दामानि प्रथयति शिलावेश्मभिर यौवनानि ||२५||

There, you should rest yourself on Nichai mountain,
Kadamba flowers would bloom with your touch
thrilled with joy, there the rock-caves
perfumed with scents of the courtesans
tell tales of debaucheries of the city men. 25

Nichai: Udaygiri hills and caves

Kadamba: Neolamarckia cadamba, an evergreen tree found in South Asia

विश्रान्तः सन व्रज वननदीतीरजानां निषिञ्चन्न
उद्यानानां नवजलकणैर यूथिकाजाल्कानि
गण्डस्वेदापनयनरुजाक्लान्तकर्णोत्पलानां
चायादानात क्षणपरिचितः पुष्पलावीमुखानाम ॥२६॥

Having rested well there, proceed, sprinkling
fresh rain drops on the Yuthika buds in the gardens
on the banks of the forest river. Enjoy a fleeting
moment with the flower girls, let your gift of shade
touch their faces, Utpala lotus on their ears have withered
sadly, soaked in sweat from their cheeks repeatedly. 26

Yuthika: fragrant jasmine

वक्रः पन्था यदपि भवतः प्रस्थितस्योत्तराशां
सौधोत्सङ्गप्रणयविमुखो मा स्म भूर उज्जयिन्याः
विद्युद्दामस्फुरितचक्रितैस तत्र पौराङ्गनानां
लोलापाङ्गैर यदि न रमसे लोचनैर वञ्चितोऽसि ॥२७॥

Although your path bound northward would be circuitous,
don't be averse to take a detour to see the palace terraces
of Ujjayini, there if you're not delighted with the eyes
of the city women, their glances trembling, frightened
by the flashes of your lightning, you're deceived. 27

वीचिक्षोभस्तनितविहगश्रेणिकाञ्चीगुणाया:
संसर्पन्त्या: स्खलितसुभगं दर्शितावर्तनाभ:
निर्विन्ध्याया: पथि भव रसाभ्यन्तर: संनिपत्य
स्त्रीणाम आद्यं प्रणयवचनं विभ्रमो हि प्रियेषु ॥२८॥

On your way, touching the waters of Nirvindhya,
her waist-band a row of birds, tinkling
with stirring of its waves, gracefully drifting,
flowing away, baring her navel—a whirlpool,
taste her water, for the first sign of craving
women to their lovers is a show of amorous play. 28

वेणीभूतप्रतनुसलिला ताम अतीतस्य सिन्धुः
पाण्डुच्छाया तटरुहतरुभ्रंशिभिर्जीर्णपर्णैः
सौभाग्यं ते सुभग विरहावस्थया व्यञ्जयन्ती
कार्श्यं येन त्यजति विधिना स त्वयैवोपपाद्यः ॥२९॥

You should find out a way to restore the river—
her scanty water appearing like a strand of hair, pale
full of withered leaves falling from the trees along her banks.
She being long parted from you, craves for your caresses. 29

प्राप्यावन्तीन उदयनकथाकोविदग्रामवृद्धान
पूर्वोद्दिष्टाम उपसर पुरीं श्रीविशालां विशालाम
स्वल्पीभूते सुचरितफले स्वर्गिणां गां गतानां
शेषैः पुण्यैर हृतम इव दिवः कान्तिमत खण्डम एकम ||३०||

When you reach Avanti, whose village elders well-versed
in the legend of Udayana, go to the magnificent city mentioned
earlier, glowing like a part of heaven brought to the earth
by those coming back from the heaven with some virtue
still left, the reserve of their virtuous deeds almost over. 30

दीर्घीकुर्वन पटु मदकलं कूजितं सारसानां
प्रत्यूषेषु स्फुटितकमलामोदमैत्रीकषाय:
यत्र स्त्रीणां हरति सुरतग्लानिम अङ्‌गानुकूल:
शिप्रावात: प्रियतम इव प्रार्थनाचाटुकार: ||३१||

Where at dawn, Sipra's cool breeze fragrant
with the perfume of opening lotuses carrying far
the piercing love cooing of sarus-cranes, caresses
the limbs of women tired from love-making,
like a lover courting his love to fulfill his desire. 31

जालोद्‌गीर्णैर उपचितवपुः केशसंस्कारधूपैर
बन्धुप्रीत्या भवनशिख्जिभिर दत्तनृत्योपहारः
हर्म्येष्व अस्याः कुसुमसुरभिष्व अधवखेदं नयेथा
लक्ष्मीं पश्यंल ललितवनितापादरागाङ्किकतेषु ॥३२॥

Your beauty enhanced by fragrance
of hair perfume wafting through the windows
and the peacocks of the palace presenting you
their dance, your soul tired with the travel, having
well-rested on flower-perfumed roofs of the palace
marked red with the feet of beautiful women 32

भर्तुः कण्ठच्छविर इति गणैः सादरं वीक्ष्यमाणः
पुण्यं यायास त्रिभुवनगुरोर धाम चण्डीश्वरस्य
धूतोद्यानं कुवलयरजोगन्धिभिर गन्धवत्यास
तोयक्रीडानिरतयुवतिस्नानतिक्तैर मरुद्भिः ॥३३॥

move on to the holy place of the Lord of three worlds—
the husband of goddess Chandi, the Ganas watching you
reverently, who see in you the beauty of their Lord's blue throat,
where the wind fragrant with blue-lotus pollen blows in
the gardens, reminiscent of the perfumes of the young girls
frolicking all the time in the waters of the river Gandhavati. 33

Shiva is the Lord of three worlds and husband of Chandi.
Ganas: Shiva's attendants

अप्य अन्यस्मिन्त्र जलधर महाकालम आसाद्य काले
स्थातव्यं ते नयनविषयं यावद अत्येति भानुः
कुर्वन सन्ध्यावलिपटहतां शूलिनः श्लाघनीयाम
आमन्द्राणां फलम अविकलं लप्स्यसे गर्जितानाम ॥३४॥

Should you reach Mahakala at any time of the day
wait till the sun sets so that you can serve
as a magnificent temple drum
during Shiva's worship at the twilight—
thus you'll relish the fruit
of your deep thundering, O Cloud! 34

पादन्यासैः क्वणितरशनास तत्र लीलावधूतै
रत्नच्छायाखचितवलिभिश चामरैः क्लान्तहस्ताः
वेश्यास त्वत्तो नखपदसुखान प्राप्य वर्षाग्रबिन्दून
आमोक्ष्यन्ते त्वयि मधुकरश्रेणिदीर्घान कटक्षान ॥३५॥

The Vesyas, whose waist-string clinks as they dance,
whose hands are tired swinging playfully chowries
with glittering gemstones studded handles,
will taste your rain-drops pleasant as a lover's nail marks
and cast on you glances, long as the rows of honeybees. 35

Vesyas: courtesans, temple-dancers
Chowries: fly-flaps made of animal tails

पश्चाद उच्चौर्भुजतरुवनं मण्डलेनाभ्लीन:
सांध्यं तेज: प्रतिनवजपापुष्परक्तं दधान:
नृत्तारम्भे हर पशुपतेर आर्द्रनागाजिनेच्चां
शान्तोद्वेगस्तिमितनयनं दृष्टभक्तिर भवान्या ||३६||

Afterwards, embrace the forest trees stretched-out like arms,
and assume the sunset glow—as red as a freshly bloomed
Japa flower—at the beginning of Shiva's cosmic dance,
dispel his desire for a blood wet elephant skin with your
devotion admired by Bhavani, her eyes steady,
her fear calmed. 36

Japa flowers: China roses

Bhavani: Shiva's wife

Legend has it that Shiva was in the habit of clothing himself in a blood wet elephant skin, which he had taken as a trophy after vanquishing a demon. His wife Bhavani disliked his filthy robe.

गच्चन्तीनां रमाणवसतिं योषितां तत्र नक्तं
रुद्धालोके नरपतिपथे सूचिभेद्यैस तमोभिः
सौदामन्या कनकनिकषस्निग्धया दर्शयोर्वीं
तोयोत्सर्गस्तनितमुहरो मा च भूर्विक्लवास्ताः ॥३७॥

Show the way to the women going to their lovers' dens at night
with your lightning, bright as a gold-streak on a touchstone,
who cannot see the path in the pitch-black darkness—
you could pierce it like a needle—but don't be noisy
with your rain and thunder, for they get easily frightened. 37

तां कस्यांचिद भवनवलभौ सुप्तपारावतायां
नीत्वा रात्रिं चिरविलसनात खिन्नविद्युत्कलत्रः
दृष्टे सूर्ये पुनरपि भवान वाहयेदध्वशेषं
मन्दायन्ते न खलु सुहृदामभ्युपतार्थकृत्याः ॥३८॥

Spend the night on some palace rooftop where doves sleep,
lightning, your wife, exhausted by continuous lovemaking,
set out on your journey at the sunrise,
for those who promise to help a friend, do not stay put. 38

तस्मिन काले नयनसलिअं योषितां खण्डितानां
शान्तिं नेयं प्रणयिभिर अतो वर्त्म भानोस त्यजाशु
प्रालेयास्त्रं कमलवदनात सोऽपि हर्तुं नलिन्याः
प्रत्यावृत्तस्त्वयि कररुधि स्यादनल्पभ्यसूयः ॥३९॥

It is the time for lovers to wipe the tears of women
jilted in love, so move out of the sun's path swiftly,
he too rises to dry dew tears from the eyes of the lotuses
and would be enraged if you obstruct his bright rays. 39

गम्भीराया: पयसि सरितश चेतसीव प्रसन्ने
चायात्मापि प्रकृतिसुभगो लप्स्यते ते प्रवेशम
तस्माद अस्या: कुमुदविशदान्य अर्हसि त्वं न धैर्यान
मोघीकर्तुं चटुलशफोरोद्वर्तनप्रेक्षितानि ||४०||

Naturally captivating, the reflection of your shadow
will enter the lucid waters of the river Gambhira,
as into a pure soul, therefore do not spurn her glances—
those agile leaps of glittering fish bright as water-lilies. 40

तस्याः किंचित्करधृतमिव प्राप्तवानीरशाखं
हृत्वा नीलं सलिलवसनं मुक्तरोधोनितम्बम
प्रस्थानं ते कथम अपि सखे लम्बमानस्य भावि
ज्ञातास्वादो विवृतजघनां को विहातुं समर्थः ॥४१॥

Like the slender arms of the lady river,
Vanira branches reach out to take away her blue
water garment and expose her thighs, the banks.
O friend, of course it would take long for you
to depart, for who has the strength to leave
a woman after relishing her bare thighs? 41

Vanira: a slender shrub

त्वन्निष्यन्दोच्छ्वसितवसुधागन्धसम्पर्करम्यः
स्रोतोरन्ध्रध्वनितसुभगं दन्तिभिः पीयमानः
नीचौर वास्यत्य उपजिगमिषोर देवपूर्वं गिरिं ते
शीतो वायुः परिणमयिता काननोदुम्बराणाम ॥४२॥

A cool breeze perfumed with Earth's fragrance,
refreshed by your showers, inhaled elegantly
by elephants, their trunks making a pleasant hum,
ripens the wild fig trees. It will blow gently
for you whenever you want to go to Devagiri. 42

तत्र स्कन्दं नियतवसतिं पुष्पमेघीकृतात्मा
पुष्पासारैः स्नपयतु भवान व्योमगङ्गाजलार्द्रैः
रक्षाहेतोर नवशशिभृता वासवीनां चमूनाम
अत्यादित्यं हुतवहमुखे संभृतं तद धि तेयः ||४३||

Skanda has made that mountain his home,
change yourself into a flower cloud
and shower him with flowers moistened
with waters of the celestial Ganges,
for his blaze surpasses even the sun's radiance,
thrown into the mouth of the divine fire
by Shiva to protect Indra's hosts. 43

Skanda, the son of Shiva and Parvati, was the war-god. Shiva, the bearer of the crescent moon, threw him in the mouth of Agni-the divine fire, Agni cast him into the Ganges, who threw him into a cavern where he lived for a 1000 years. Later he killed a demon who frightened Indra's hosts.

ज्योतिर्लेखावलयि गलितं यस्य बर्हं भवानी
पुत्रप्रेम्णा कुवलयदलप्रापि कर्णे करोति
धौतापाङ्गं हरशशिरुचा पावकेस तं मयूरं
पश्चाद अद्रिग्रहणगुरुभिर गर्जितैर नर्तयेथाः ॥४४॥

Afterwards, let your heavy rolling thunder
magnified by mountain-echoes make the peacocks dance
whose eye-corners radiate white under the glow of Hara's moon,
whose moulted tail feathers studded with stars adorn Bhavani's
ears in place of blue lotus petals, for the love of her son. 44

Hara: an early name of Shiva

Skanda is Bhavani's son, and is represented as seated on a peacock with white eyes.

आराध्यैनं शरवणभवं देवम उल्लङ्घिताध्वा
सिद्धद्वन्द्वैर जलकणभयाद वीणिभिर मुक्तमार्ग:
व्यालम्बेथा: सुरभितनयालम्भजां मानयिष्यन
स्रोतोमूर्त्या भुवि परिणतां रन्तिदेवस्य कीर्तिम ॥४५॥

Having pleased that reed-wood-born god,
advance on your path, the lute-bearing Siddhas
will leave your path free fearing your rain-drops,
yet stop by to praise the glory of Rantideva
sprung from the slaughter of Surabhi's daughters,
flowing on earth transformed into a stream. 45

Reed-wood-born god is Skanda. The Siddhas, who amuse Skanda with their lutes, will get out of the way for fear of having their lute-strings relaxed by rain-drops.

As per the legend, Surabhi or Kamdhenu, a cow of plenty gave birth to many golden cows collectively known as Kapila.

त्वय्य आदातुं जलम अवनते शाङ्गिर्णो वर्णचौरे
तस्याः सिन्धोः पृथुम अपि तनुं दूरभावात प्रवाहम
प्रेक्षिष्यन्ते गगनगतयो नूनम आवर्ज्य दृष्टिर
एकं भुक्तागुणम इव भुवः स्थूलमध्येन्द्रनीलम ||४६||

Stealing Vishnu's colour, when you bow to drink water
the Siddhas will surely look at you with awe,
the broad stream of river will appear narrow from far
as if the earth is wearing a beautiful pearl necklace
with a large sapphire in the middle. 46

Vishnu: god who carries horn-bow
Siddhas: sky travellers

ताम उत्तीर्य व्रज परिचितभ्रूलताविभ्रमाणां
पक्ष्मोत्क्षेपाद उपरिविलसत्कृष्णशारप्रभाणाम
कुन्दक्षेपानुगमधुकरश्रीमुषाम आत्मबिम्बं
पात्रीकुर्वन दशपुरवधूनेत्रकौतूहलानाम ॥४७॥

Keep going onwards, women's eyelashes
flutter like leaves as they raise their eyebrows,
glittering with black radiance, stealing the beauty
of honey-bees hovering around Kunda flowers,
their curious eyes will follow you crossing the river. 47

Kunda: Downy Jasmine

ब्रह्मावर्तं जनपदम अथ च्चायया गाहमान:
क्षेत्रं क्षत्रप्रधनपिशुनं कौरवं तद भजेथा:
राजन्यानां शितशरशतैर यत्र गाण्डीवधन्वा
धारापातैस त्वम इव कमलान्य अभ्यवर्षन मुखानि ॥४८॥

Your shadow spread over the land of Brahmavarta,
visit the battlefield of Kurukshetra, the place of the great war
of Mahabharata, where Arjuna showered the heads of princes
with hundreds of arrows as you shower raindrops on lotuses. 48

Kurukshetra : where the great war of Mahabharata was fought
Arjuna: the wielder of Gandiva, a special bow

हित्वा हालाम अभिमतरसां रेवतीलोचनाङ्कां
बन्धुप्रीत्या समरविमुखो लाङ्गली याः सिषेवे
कृत्वा तासाम अधिगमम अपां सौम्य सारस्वतीनाम
अन्तः शुद्धस त्वम अपि भविता वर्णमात्रेण कृष्णः ||४९||

Balrama—the plough bearer gave up his favourite wine
resembling Revati's eyes, for the sake of his people, and
renounced war, worshipping Saraswati's waters.
O gentle soul, drinking her waters, dark only in colour,
you'll become pure within. 49

The ploughbearer Balrama and his wife Revati were addicted to drinking. When the great war of Mahabharata broke out, Balarama, being friend of both Pandava and Kaurava, retired to the banks of Saraswati. A visit to its waters was supposed to cleanse them from all sins.

तस्माद गच्चेर अनुकनखलं शैलराजावतीर्णां
जाह्नोः कन्यां सगरतनयस्वर्गसोपानपङ्क्तिम
गौरीवक्त्रभ्रुकुटिरचनां या विहस्येव फेनैः
शम्भोः केशग्रहणम अकरोद इन्दुलग्नोर्मिहस्ता ||५०||

From there go to visit Jahnu's daughter
descended from the Himalayas near Kanakhala
—the stairway to heaven for Sagar's sons.
She, laughing at frowning Gauri with her frothing foam
seizes Shiva's hair, her wave-hands holding on to the moon. 50

Jahnu's daughter: the Ganges

Kanakhala: Hardvar

Legend has it that the Ganges was brought down from the heaven by long and pious austerity of Bhagiratha, the son of Sagar to wash the ashes of 60,000 sons of Sagar, who ascended to heaven through her. As the Earth would not have been able to bear the sudden descent of such a great river, Shiva offered to let her fall on his head. Gauri, his wife, became jealous seeing the Ganges play with her husband's hair.

तस्याः पातुं सुरगज इव व्योम्नि पश्चार्धलम्बी
त्वं चेद अच्चस्फटिकविशदं तर्कयेस तिर्यग अम्भः
संसर्पन्त्या सपदि भवतः स्रोतसि च्चाययासौ
स्याद अस्थानोपगतयमुनासंगमेवाभिरामा ॥५१॥

If you, like a celestial elephant, having your front half
bowing down, think to drink her crystal clear waters
as your shadow glides gently over the river, it would be
exquisite, as if Ganga and Yamuna flowed there together. 51

आसीनानां सुरभितशिलं नाभिगन्धैर मृगाणां
तस्या एव प्रभवम अचलं प्राप्य गौरं तुषारैः
वक्ष्यस्य अध्वश्रमविनयेन तस्य शृङ्गे निषण्णः
शोभां शुभ्रां त्रिनयनवृषोत्खातपङ्कोपमेयम ॥५२॥

Having arrived at her birthplace in the Himalayas
whose rocks are perfumed with the navel-scent
of the musk deer reclining there on one
of its fatigue-removing peaks, you'll appear
like a scraped-up black earth on the horn
of handsome Nandi of the three-eyed-one. 52

The Ganges originates from the Himalayan glaciers. Three-eyed-one is Lord Shiva and Nandi, his white bull.

तं चेद् वायौ सरति सरलस्कन्धसंघट्टजन्मा
बाधेतोल्काक्षपितचमरीबालभारो दवाग्निः
अर्हस्य एनं शमयितुम अलं वारिधारासहस्रैर
आपन्नार्तिप्रशमनफलाः संपदो ह्य उत्तमानाम ॥५३॥

When the wind blows in the mountains
the bushy tails of Chamari yaks may catch fire
from the bushfire caused by the thick trunks of Sarala
rubbing against each other, please quench it by your rain-showers,
for the riches of those endowed by fortune are best
used to alleviate the suffering of those in distress. 53

Sarala: a tall, coniferous pine

ये संरम्भोत्पतनरभसाः स्वाङ्गभङ्गाय तस्मिन
मुक्ताध्वानं सपदि शरभा लङ्घयेयुर भवन्तम
तान कुर्वीथास तुमुलकरकावृष्टिपातावकीर्णन
के वा न स्युः परिभवपदं निष्फलारम्भयत्नाः ॥५४॥

The Sarabhas, unable to bear your thundering,
full of pride, will try to leap over you, only to shatter
their bodies. You're unsurmountable. Astonish them
with your loud laughter of hailstorm and rain,
for whoever takes a vainglorious enterprise
becomes a laughing stock! 54

The Sarabhas, according to the legends, were eight-legged animals, inhabiting the high Himalayas. They impossibly attempted to leap over the clouds.

तत्र व्यंक्तं दृषदि चरणन्यासमर्धेन्दुमौले:
शश्वत् सिद्धैरुपहृतबलिं भक्तिनम्र: परीया:
यस्मिन् दृष्टे करणविगमादूर्ध्वमुद्धूतपापा:
संकल्पन्ते स्थिरगणपदप्राप्तये श्रद्दधाना: ॥५५॥

There, in a reverent posture, circumambulate the rock
bearing the footprint of Shiva, continually worshipped
by the Siddhas with sacrifice. The believers, seeing it,
get absolved of their sins and find eternal home there
as Ganas, after abandoning their bodies. 55

Circumambulation or Dakshina is a religious ceremony practiced among the Hindus. Shiva is the crescent moon bearing god and Ganas are his attendants.

शब्दायन्ते मधुरम अनिलैः कीचकाः पूर्यमाणाः
संरक्ताभिस त्रिपुरविजयो गीयते किंनराभिः
निर्ह्लादस ते मुरज इव चेत कन्दरेषु ध्वनिः स्यात
संगीतार्थो ननु पशुपतेस तत्र भावी समग्रः ॥५६॥

Hollow Kichakas make sweet sound, wind running through
them, Kinnaris sing passionately the paeans of triumph
over Tripura, your thunder rumbles like a Muraja drum
in the cavern,completing Pashupati's mighty orchestra. 56

Kichaka: thorny bamboo (Bambusa arundinacea)

Kinnaris: wood nymphs, the Kinnaris were the wives of the Kinnaras, the followers of Kubera, the god of wealth

Tripura: a demon slain by Ravana

प्रालेयाद्रेर उपतटम अतिक्रम्य तांस तान विशेषान
हंसद्वारं भृगुपतियशोवर्त्म यत क्रौञ्चरन्ध्रम
तेनोदीचीं दिशम अनुसरेस तिर्यग आयामशोभी
श्यामः पादो बलिनियमनाभ्युद्यतस्येव विष्णोः ||५७||

Having passed over various Himalyan slopes
you should take the northern route
through the celebrated Krauncha pass—
the gate for the Hansas, the famed path
of Bhrigupati—stretched horizontally,
shining like the dark-blue foot of Vishnu
prepared to humble Bali's pride. 57

The legend of Krauncha or Niti pass, Bhrigupati's famed path finds mention is Vishnu Purana. Bhrigupati opened the pass by shooting an arrow through which the Hansas or the wild geese, pass to the Manasa lake. Vishnu reincarnated himself to free the world from the tyranny of giant Bali. He raised his foot to crush him but stopped short of it upon Bali's submission.

गत्वा चोर्ध्वं दशमुखभुजोच्छ्वासितप्रस्थसंधेः
कैलासस्य त्रिदशवनितादर्पणस्यातिथिः स्याः
शृङ्गोच्छ्रायैः कुमुदविशदैर यो वितत्य स्थितः खं
राशीभूतः प्रतिदिनम इव त्र्यम्बकस्यट्टहासः ॥५८॥

Soaring above, be the guest of Mount Kailasa—
shaken violently by Ravana's mighty arms,
—the celestial nymphs' mirror, its lofty peaks
like moon-lotuses shooting forth into the heavens
like bursts of Shiva's laughter piercing the universe. 58

Ravana: the ten headed demon who tried to displace Mount Kailasa but didn't succeed

Shiva: three-eyed god whose abode is Mount Kailasa

उत्पश्यामि त्वयि तटगते स्निग्धभिन्नाञ्जनाभे
सद्यः कृत्तद्विरददशनच्चेदगौरस्य तस्य
शोभाम अद्रेः स्तिमितनयनप्रेक्षणीयां भवित्रीम
अंसन्यस्ते सति हलभृतो मेचके वाससीव ॥५९॥

You shine like collyrium, leaning on the
mountain slopes—white as freshly cut ivory,
the Himalayas will attain exquisite grandeur
like the plough-bearer Balrama wearing
two dark-blue garments on his shoulders. 59

हित्वा तस्मिन भुजगवलयं शम्भुना दत्तहस्ता
क्रीडाशैले यदि च विचरेत्पादचारेण गौरी
भङ्गीभक्त्या विरचितवपुः स्तम्भितान्तर्जलौघः
सोपानत्वं कुरु मणितटारोहणायाग्रयायी ||६०||

If Gauri were to take a stroll on this pleasure mountain
holding Shiva's hand, having kept aside her snake bracelet,
transform yourself into wave-step controlling water flow
within you—a staircase fit for their climb. 60

तत्रावश्यं वलयकुलिशोद्धट्टनोद्गीर्णतोयं
नेष्यन्ति त्वां सुरयुवतयो यन्त्रधारागृहत्वम
ताभ्यो मोक्षस तव यदि सखे घर्मलब्धस्य न स्यात
क्रीडालोला: श्रवणपरुषैर गर्जितैर भाययेस ता: ॥६१॥

Undoubtedly, as by gentle tinkling of diamond
bracelets as by thunderbolts, your rain would
be ejected, showering the young sky maidens.
O friend, seized by passion, if you're not able
to leave, if they are still eager to frolick with
you, frighten them by your roaring thunder. 61

According to a legend, the thunderbolts and diamonds are composed of the same material. The thunder is expected to make the clouds release rain. The diamond bracelets of the young sky maidens are expected to do the same.

हेमाम्भोजप्रसवि सलिलं मानसस्याददानः
कुर्वन कामं क्षणमुखपटप्रीतिम ऐरावतस्य
धुन्वन कल्पद्रुमकिसलयान यंशुकानीव वातैर
नानाचेष्टैर जलदललितैर निर्विशेस तं नगेन्द्रम ॥६२॥

Sip Manasa's water where golden lotuses bloom,
offer Airavata the pleasure of shade or as you like,
shake the fine white garments of Kalpataru
with rain-laden breeze, enjoy playing the game
of light and shadow with the crystal-white peaks. 62

Airavata is the celestial elephant.
The Kalpataru is the wish fulfilling tree of the heaven as they grant everything wished for.

तस्योत्सङ्गे प्रणयिन इव स्रस्तगङ्गादुकूलां
न त्वं दृष्ट्वा न पुनर अलकां ज्ञास्यसे कामचारिन
या वः काले वहति सलिलोद्गारम उच्चौर विमाना
मुक्ताजालग्रथितम अलकं कामिनीवाभ्रवृन्दम ॥६३॥

O wanderer at will, seeing Alaka
you'll certainly recognize her seated
on Mount Kailasa, in her lover's lap,
her white garment—the Ganges, fallen off.
In the rainy-season, a mass of rain-clouds
adorn her lofty palaces, like pearl strings
gracing the hair of lovely women. 63

Alaka, lying on the slopes of Kailasa is imagined to be Mount Kailasa's beloved, her garment the river Ganges slipped off so that her beauty is exposed to be admired.

विधुन्वन्तं ललितवनिता: सेन्द्रचापं सचित्रा:
संगीताय प्रहतमुरजा: स्निग्धगम्भीरघोषम
अन्तस्तोयं मणिमयभुवस तुङ्गम अभ्रंलिहाग्रा:
प्रासादास त्वां तुलयितुम अलं यत्र तैस तैर विशेषै: ||६४||

Where palaces, kissing the sky, can match
your splendour, one on one, on each of these—
terraces made of precious stones rival the sparkle
of your radiant rain drops, murals on the walls
compete with the colours of your rainbow, flirty
women rival lightning's playfulness, and the beating
of drums match the deep-throated sound of your thunder. 64

हस्ते लीलाकमलम अलके बालकुन्दानुविद्धं
नीता रोध्रप्रसवरजसा पाण्डुताम आनने श्री:
चूडापाशे नवकुरवकं चारु कर्णे शिरीषं
सीमन्ते च त्वदुपगमजं यत्र नीपं वधूनाम ॥६५॥

There, a woman plays with a red lotus in her hand,
freshly bloomed Kunda in her hair, her graceful face
painted fair with the pollen of Rodhra, her braid tied
with fresh Kurabaka, Sirisa in her pretty ears, and Nipa
at her hair-parting, all blossomed upon your arrival. 65

All the flowers mentioned here have a special season to blossom as per Ritusamhara by Kalidasa. Kunda in Autumn, Rodhra in Winter, Kurabaka in Spring, Sirisa in Summer and Nipa blossoms in the rainy season. All these blossom together at once in Alaka.

यस्यां यक्षाः सितमणिमयान्य एत्य हर्म्यस्थलानि
ज्योतिश्चायाकुसुमरचितान्य उत्तमस्त्रीसहायाः
आसेवन्ते मधु रतिफलं कल्पवृक्षप्रसूतं
त्वद्गम्भीरध्वनिषु शनकैः पुष्करेष्व आहतेषु ॥६६॥

Where Yakshas with charming women as companions,
revel on their palace-terraces paved with moonstones
resembling flowers under starlight, addicting themselves
to Ratiphala wine pressed from Kalpataru, Puskara drums
beating gently producing deep and soft sound like yours. 66

Ratiphala: an aphrodisiac fruit
Kalpataru: wish fulfilling tree

गत्युत्कम्पादलकपतितैर्यत्रमन्दारपुष्पैः
क्ऌप्तच्छेद्यैः कनककमलैःकर्णविभ्रंशिभिश्च।
मुक्तालग्नस्तनपरिमलैश्छिन्नसूत्रैश्च हारैर्
नैशो मार्गः सवितुरुदये सूच्यते कामिनीनाम् ॥६७॥

Where at the dawn, the night-path of the amorous women
is revealed by fallen Mandara flowers from their ringlets,
golden lotuses torn, fallen from their ears,
threads of their necklaces broken, pearls scattered,
fragrant from the perfume of their breasts. 67

Mandara: Erythrina variegata or Indian coral tree

नीवीबन्धोच्च्वासितशिथिलं यत्र बिम्बाधराणां
क्षौमं रागादनिभृतकरेष्व आक्षिपत्सु प्रियेषु
अर्चिस्तुङ्गान अभिमुखम अपि प्राप्य रत्नप्रदीपान
ह्रीमूढानां भवति विफलप्रेरणा चूर्णमुष्टिः ||६८||

When the lovers, full of desire, with their impudent
hands undo the waist-string and toss aside
the slackened silk garments of Yaksha women,
who, covered in shame, throw a handful of churna
on the jewel lamps with high flames. Ah! but in vain! 68

Churna: aromatic powder

नेत्रा नीताः सततगतिना यद्विमानाग्रभूमीर
आलेख्यानां सलिलकणिकादोषम उत्पाद्य सद्यः
शङ्कास्पृष्टा इव जलमुचस त्वादृशा जालमार्गैर
धूमोद्गारानुकृतिनिपुणा जर्जरा निष्पतन्ति ॥६९॥

Where, clouds resembling you, led by the ever blowing
wind to the high palace floors, spoil the paintings
with water-droplets and escape through the lattices, as if
by fear, being skilled in imitating the shapes of smoke. 69

यत्र स्त्रीणां प्रियतमभुजोच्छ्वासितालिङ्गितानाम
अङ्गग्लानिं सुरतजनितां तन्तुजालावलम्बाः
त्वत्संरोधापगमविशदश चन्द्रपादैर निशीथे
व्यालुम्पन्ति स्फुटजललवस्यन्दिनश चन्द्रकान्ताः ||७०||

Where at midnight, moonstones, hanging
from the thread nets, touched by the moonbeams,
free from your obstruction, ooze drops of cool water
and take away the weariness of women
released from the arms of their lovers
after hours of lovemaking. 70

According to a legend, Chandrakanta or Moonstone is capable of absorbing the Moon rays and then exuding cool water.

मत्वा देवं धनपतिसखं यत्र साक्षाद वसन्तं
प्रायश चापं न वहति भयान मन्मथ: षट्पदज्यम
सभ्रूभङ्गप्रहितनयनै: कामिलक्ष्येष्व अमोघैस
तस्यारम्भश चतुरवनिताविभ्रमैर एव सिद्धः ॥७१॥

Where Shiva, friend of Kubera, himself lives—
and fearing him the god of love does not bear
his bow strung with bees, his work accomplished
by charming women whose arched eyebrows
like stretched bows shoot seductive looks
at the lovers—their preys. 71

Shiva: the supreme god
Kubera: the Lord of wealth
The legend has it that Manmatha, the god of love was afraid of Shiva having once been reduced to ashes by his fiery glance.

तत्रागारं धनपतिगृहान उत्तरेणास्मदीयं
दूराल लक्ष्यं सुरपतिधनुश्चारुणा तोरणेन
यस्योपान्ते कृतकतनयः कान्तया वर्धितो मे
हस्तप्राप्यस्तवकनमितो बालमन्दारवृक्षः ||७२||

There, to the north of the Kubera's palace, is my dwelling
recognizable from far by its ornate arched gate
resembling a rainbow and a young Mandara tree,
like an adopted son to me, leans to his mother,
so my love's hands can touch his blossoms. 72

Mandara: Erithrina fulgens or stricta, a red flower considered to be found in the gardens of Indra in Hindu mythology

वापी चास्मिन मरकतशिलाबद्धसोपानमार्गा
हैमैश्चन्ना विकचकमलैः स्निग्धवैदूर्यनालैः
यस्यास तोये कृतवसतयो मानसं संनिकृष्टं
नाध्यास्यन्ति व्यपगतशुचस त्वाम अपि प्रेक्ष्य हंसाः ||७३||

From there, a flight of stairs made of emerald
leads to an oblong pond covered with golden lotuses
with glossy stalks like lapis lazuli. The Hansas
seeing you there,will put aside their regrets,
and stop craving for the nearby Manasa. 73

Hansas: Swans

तस्यास तीरे रचितशिखरः पेशलैर इन्द्रनीलैः
क्रीडाशैलः कनककदलीवेष्टनप्रेक्षणीयः
मद्गेहिन्याः प्रिय इति सखे चेतसा कातरेण
प्रेक्ष्योपान्तस्फुरिततडितं त्वां तम एव स्मरामि ||७४||

On its bank, a crafted pleasure hill,
its crest made of Indranila sapphires
enclosed by a fence of golden Kadalis,
is breathtaking and my wife's favourite!
O friend, when you appear with your lightning
and thunder, that very spot flashes in my anxious mind. 74

रक्ताशोकश चलकिसलय: केसरश चात्र कान्त:
प्रत्यासन्नौ कुरुवकवृतेर माधवीमण्डपस्य
एक: सख्यास तव सह मया वामपादाभिलाषी
काङ्‌क्षत्य अन्यो वदनमदिरां दोहदच्चद्मनास्या: ||७५||

The red Ashoka's tender leaves flutter, Kesara looks lovely
next to the hedge of Kurabakas and the grove of Madhavi,
one longs for the left foot of my love, just like me,
another craves for the kiss of her mouth
pretending it's time to bloom. 75

As per the legend, the Ashoka tree only blossoms when touched by the foot of a beautiful woman, and the Kesara only when kissed by her lips.
Madhavi: a kind of Jasmine
Kurubakas: amaranth hedge

तन्मध्ये च स्फटिकफलका काञ्चनी वासयष्टिर
मूले बद्धा मणिभिर अनतिप्रौढवंशप्रकाशैः
तालैः शिञ्जावलयसुभगैर नर्तितः कान्तया मे
याम अध्यास्ते दिवसविगमे नीलकण्ठः सुहृद वः ॥७६॥

Among these trees, a golden pillar rises
perched on a pedestal of crystals,
its base studded with emeralds
glittering like freshly sprouted bamboos—
there at the end of the day,
the blue-necked peacock, your friend,
alights and dances at the sweet tinkling
of my wife's bracelets when she claps her hands. 76

Artificial pillars were made for the peacocks to roost at night. The precious stones like emeralds, resembling verdure were put to attract the birds.

एभिः साधो हृदयनिहितैर लक्षणैर लक्षयेथा
द्वारोपान्ते लिखितवपुषौ शङ्खपद्मौ च दृष्ट्वा
क्षामच्चायां भवनम अधुना मद्वियोगेन नूनं
सूर्यापाये न खलु कमलं पुष्यति स्वामभिख्याम ||७७||

By these clues treasured in your heart,
noticing the beautifully painted figures
of lotus and conch on the doors,
O friend, you'll certainly recognize my house,
its glimmer slightly faded in my absence
for the lotus loses its beauty after the sunset. 77

Conch and lotus are two of the nine treasures of Kubera, the lord of wealth. Conch is used in religious ceremonies and once was a source of considerable revenue for the treasury.

गत्वा सद्यः कलभतनुतां शीघ्रसंपातहेतोः
क्रीडाशैले प्रथमकथिते रम्यसानौ निषण्णः
अर्हस्य अन्तर्भवनपतितां कर्तुम अल्पाल्पभासं
खद्योतालीविलसितनिभां विद्युदुन्मेषदृष्टिम ॥७८॥

Assuming the form of a baby elephant for a swift descent,
reclining on the pleasure mountain with a sapphire crest
as mentioned earlier, open your lightning-eye to make a faint
flash like a swarm of fireflies flying into the house. 78

The cloud is urged to reduce its size in order to not to frighten Yaksha's wife.

तन्वी श्यामा शिखरीदशना पक्वबिम्बाधरौष्ठी
मध्ये क्षामा चकितहरिणीप्रेक्षणा निम्ननाभिः
श्रोणीभाराद अलसगमना स्तोकनम्रा स्तनाभ्यां
या तत्र स्याद युवतीविषये सृष्टिराद्येव धातुः ||७९||

Her body dusky, delicate, her teeth like jasmine buds,
her lips ripe bimba fruits, her eyes like a startled deer's,
she is thin in the middle, her navel deep,
she walks slowly from the heaviness of her hips,
and bends forward a bit because of her breasts—
she is like Brahma's first creation among the women. 79

Bimba fruit: Coccinia Grandis
Brahma: creator god in Hinduism

तां जानीथा: परिमितकथां जीवितं मे द्वितीयं
दूरीभूते मयि सहचरे चक्रवाकीम इवैकाम
गाढोत्कण्ठां गुरुषु दिवसेष्व एषु गच्चत्सु बालां
जातां मन्ये शिशिरमथितां पद्मिनीं वान्यरूपाम ||८०||

You may know, she is my second self—
home alone, resembling the lonesome Chakravaki,
she hardly talks—separated from her love,
with the passing of these difficult days,
anguished by intense craving, my young wife
would have changed much, I imagine,
like a lotus bitten by frost in the long winter. 80

The Chakravaki bird, according to the legend, was cursed by Rama to be separated from her mate every night.

नूनं तस्याः प्रबलरुदितोच्चूननेत्रं प्रियाया
निःश्वासानाम अशिशिरतया भिन्नवर्णाधरोष्ठम
हस्तन्यस्तं मुखम असकलव्यक्ति लम्बालकत्वाद
इन्दोर दैन्यं त्वदनुसरणक्लिष्टकान्तेर बिभर्ति ॥८१॥

Surely her eyes would be swollen
from violent weeping and the colour
of her lips pale with her hot sighs,
her face placed in her cupped palms
not clearly visible through her hair
like the miserable state of the moon,
when her glow is obscured by you. 81

आलोके ते निपतति पुरा सा बलिव्याकुला वा
मत्सादृश्यं विरहतनु वा भावगम्यं लिखन्ती
पृच्चन्ती वा मधुरवचनां सारिकां पञ्जरस्थां
कच्चिद भर्तुः स्मरसि रसिके त्वं हि तस्य प्रियेति ॥८२॥

When you see her, she will be either engaged
actively in the daily worship rituals, or picturing
my resemblance—emaciated by separation,
or asking Sarika, the melodious Maina in the cage—
"Surely you remember your lord, lonely one,
for truly you're his love." 82

Sarika: a common talking Maina, Gracula religiosa

उत्सङ्गे वा मलिनवसने सौम्य निक्षिप्य वीणां
मद्गोत्राङ्कं विरचितपदं गेयम उद्गातुकामा
तन्त्रीम आर्द्रां नयनसलिलैः सारयित्वा कथंचिद
भूयो भूयः स्वयम अपि कृतां मूर्च्छनां विस्मरन्ती ॥८३॥

Or, placing a Veena on her shabbily-clothed thigh
wishing to sing a song composed for me
making the strings wet with her tears—
so that they vibrate somehow or the other,
O dear, she forgets the tunes again and again
even though she has composed them herself. 83

Dirty garments were a sign of sorrow.
Veena: a four stringed instrument

शेषान मासान विरहदिवासस्थापितस्यावधेर वा
विन्यस्यन्ती भुवि गणनया देहलीदत्तपुष्पैः
सम्भोगं वा हृदयनिहितारम्भम आस्वादयन्ती
प्रायेणैते रमणविरहेष्व अङ्गनानां विनोदाः ॥८४॥

Or she is counting the remaining months
of our separation by arranging flowers
thrown down on the floor from the balcony
or rejoicing in imagined pleasures of our
reunion treasured in her heart—for these are
pastimes of women parted from their lovers. 84

It was a practice among women to hang up flowers for the number of days or months their lovers or husbands were to be absent. Then they threw them on the ground, one by one, to count the days left of their reunion.

सव्यापारम अहनि न तथा पीडयेद विप्रयोग:
शङ्के रात्रौ गुरुतरशुचं निर्विनोदां सखीं ते
मत्सन्देश: सुखयितुम अलं पश्य साध्वीं निशीथे
ताम उन्निद्राम अवनिशयनां सौधवातायनस्थ: ||८५||

My absence may not distress her so much,
she keeps busy during the day, but at night, I fear
your friend, with nothing to do, suffers greatly
in grief. So, stand close to the window to see
my sweet wife lying awake on the floor,
cheer her up with my message at midnight. 85

आधिक्षामां विरहशयने संनिषण्णैकपार्श्वां
प्राचीमूले तनुम इव कलामात्रशेषां हिमांशोः
नीता रात्रिः क्षण इव मया सार्धम इच्चारतैर या
ताम एवोष्णैर विरहमहतीम अश्रुभिर यापयन्तीम ॥८६॥

She may be flung on her side of the lonely bed
from mental agony, slender like the waning moon
on the eastern horizon, only one sixteenth
of its diameter left, passing the long night
in separation with hot tears trickling down
her eyes—which once passed in moments
making love whenever we wanted. 86

नि:श्वासेनाधरकिसलयक्लेशिना विक्षिपन्तीं
शुद्धस्नानात परुषमलकं नूनमागण्डलम्बम
मत्संभोगः कथमुपनमेत स्वप्नजोऽपीति निद्राम
आकाङ्‌क्षन्तीं नयनसलिलोत्पीडरुद्धावकाशम ॥८७॥

Her lip buds hurting with hot sighs,
you'll see her tossing aside her hair—
rough from frequent ritual bathing,
hanging carelessly on her cheeks
hoping for a rendezvous with me,
at least in dreams, she longs to sleep
but for hot teardrops trickling from her eyes. 87

आद्ये बद्धा विरहदिवसे या शिखा दाम हित्वा
शापस्यान्ते विगलितशुचा तां मयोद्वेष्टनीयाम
स्पर्शक्लिष्टाम अयमितनखेनासकृत्सारयन्तीं
गण्डाभोगात कठिनविषमाम एकवेणीं करेण ॥८८॥

I'll untie the Veni she tied on the day of our parting
when my curse gets over and suffering ends,
she flings it frequently with her hands,
her nails neglected, whenever her Veni
hard and rough, falls painfully on her face. 88

Veni or the top-knot of hair tied by the women whenever their husbands set out on journey.

पादान इन्दोरमृतशिशिराञ्जलमार्गप्रविष्टान
पूर्वप्रीत्या गतमभुमुखं संनिवृत्तं तथैव
चक्षुः खेदात सलिलगुरुभिः पक्ष्मभिश्चादयन्तीं
साभ्रेऽह्नीव स्थलकमलिनी न प्रभुद्धां न सुप्ताम ||८९||

Her eyes, which used to turn towards
the moonbeam—cool, life-giving like Amrita
gushing in through the windows, during our lovemaking,
she now covers them and withdraws from weariness,
her eyes full of tears like the land lotus
on a cloudy day, half asleep, half awake 89

Amrita: elixir

It is a popular belief that Moonlight delights in the presence of a lover but causes immense pain during his/her absence.

Land Lotus: Hibiscus mutabilis

सा संन्यस्ताभरणम अबला पेशलं धारयन्ती
शय्योत्सङ्गे निहितम असकृद दुःखदुःखेन गात्रम
त्वाम अप्य अस्रं नवजलमयं मोचयिष्यत्य अवश्यं
प्रायः सर्वो भवति करुणावृत्तिर आर्द्रान्तरात्मा ||९०||

Discarding all her ornaments,
wearing only her intense misery,
her body on the bed's edge,
my young and delicate wife
will make you cry with rain drops,
for the soft-hearts easily melt. 90

जाने सख्यास तव मयि मनः संभृतस्नेहमस्माद
इत्थंभूतां प्रथमविरहे ताम अहं तर्कयामि
वाचालं मां न खलु सुभगंमन्यभावः करोति
प्रत्यक्षं ते निखिलम अचिराद भ्रातर उक्तं मया यत ॥९१॥

I know that my wife's heart is full of love for me
this being our first separation, so I presume,
she has become like this. I don't feel happy
to boast it all, you'll soon see it for yourself
O friend, all that I have just said. 91

रुद्धापाङ्गप्रसरम अलकैर अञ्जनस्नेहशून्यं
प्रत्यादेशाद अपि च मधुनो विस्मृतभ्रूविलासम
त्वय्य आसन्ने नयनम उपरिस्पन्दि शङ्के मृगाक्ष्या
मीनक्षोभाच चलकुवलयश्रीतुलाम एष्यतीति ॥९२॥

Her eyes kohl-less, side glances blocked by stray hair,
her brow play forgotten with abstinence from wine—
the doe-eyed beauty's left eye would twitch upward
on your arrival, as a blue lotus quivers
from the touch of a fish. 92

The twitching of the left eye or throbbing, pulsation or quivering of the left thigh in women was considered to be a sign of luck.

वामश चास्याः कररुहपदैर मुच्यमानो मदीयैर
मुक्ताजालं चिरपरिचितं त्याजितो दैवगत्या
संभोगान्ते मम समुचितो हस्तसंवाहमानां
यास्यत्य ऊरुः सरसकदलीस्तम्भगौरश चलत्वम ॥९३॥

Her left thigh free from claw marks of my nails,
deprived of long-worn pearl chain by the turn of fate,
used to soft rubbing of my hand after making love,
like the pale stem of fresh Kadali, will start quivering. 93

Her thigh has become pale from grief of separation. The act of soft rubbing by hand is expected to take away her weariness after making love.

Kadali: Plantain

तस्मिन काले जलद यदि सा लब्धनिद्रासुखा स्याद
अन्वास्यैनां स्तनितविमुखो याममात्रं सहस्व
मा भूद अस्याः प्रणयिनि मयि स्वप्नलब्धे कथंचित
सद्यः कण्ठच्युतभुजलताग्रन्थि गाढोपगूढम ॥९४॥

O rainmaker, if at that time, she has gone off to sleep,
wait there floating, withholding your thunder, wait
a bit until she sees me—her lover, in her dreams,
so that you don't make her lose the firm grasp
of her tender creeper like arms around my neck. 94

ताम उत्थाप्य स्वजलकणिकाशीतलेनानिलेन
प्रत्याश्वस्तां समम अभिनवैर जालकैर मालतीनाम
विद्युद्गर्भः स्तिमितनयनां त्वत्सनाथे गवाक्षे
वक्तुं धीरः स्तनितवचनैर मानिनीं प्रक्रमेथाः ॥९५॥

Aroused by cool breeze from your drizzling,
refreshed with the tender buds of jasmine,
start addressing her by a deep-sounding speech
standing near the window, her eyes on you
with your mild lightning flash. 95

भर्तुर मित्रं प्रियम अविधवे विद्धि माम अम्बुवाहं
तत्संदेशैर हृदयनिहितैर आगतं त्वत्समीपम
यो वृन्दानि त्वरयति पथि श्रम्यतां प्रोषितानां
मन्द्रस्निग्धैर ध्वनिभिर अबलावेणिमोक्षोत्सुकानि ॥९६॥

O noble lady, I'm a rain cloud, a dear friend
of your husband, carrying his words etched in my heart.
My pleasant rumblings prod the weary travellers
to hurry home to unknot the Venis of their women. 96

Veni or the top-knot of hair tied by the women whenever their husbands set out on journey.

The sight of the Cloud was sufficient to urge the tired travellers and to inspire them to continue their journey.

इत्य आख्याते पवनतनयं मैथिलीवोन्मुखी सा
त्वाम उत्कण्ठोच्च्वसितहृदया वीक्ष्य सम्भाव्य चौव
श्रोष्यत्य अस्मात परम अवहिता सौम्य सीमन्तिनीनां
कान्तोदन्तः सुहृदुपनतः संगमात किंचिद ऊनः ॥९७॥

Thus with bated breath, her heart opening
like a lotus hearing this news, having received
and honoured you, like Hanuman by Sita,
O friend, she will listen to you attentively,
for women the news of their husbands delivered
by a friend is nothing less than returning home. 97

Sita or Maithali is another name of Rama's wife. When Sita was abducted by Ravana to Lanka, Hanuman, son of the wind, brought her news of Rama, and she honoured him.

ताम आयुष्मन मम च वचनाद आत्मनश चोपकर्तुं
ब्रूया एवं तव सहचरो रामगिर्याश्रमस्थः
अव्यापन्नः कुशलम अबले पृच्चति त्वां वियुक्तः
पूर्वाभाष्यं सुलभविपदां प्राणिनाम एतद एव ॥९८॥

O long-lived one! to fulfill my request please tell her—
"your husband is alive, living at hermitages in Ramagiri,
not quite dead yet, separated from you. He asks if all is well
with you, O tender lady!" For those alive should be addressed
tenderly as they are prone to fall to calamity easily. 98

अङ्गेनाङ्गं प्रतनु तनुना गाढतप्तेन तप्तं
सास्रेणाश्रुद्रुतम अविरतोत्कण्ठम उत्कण्ठितेन
उष्णोच्च्वासं समधिकतरोच्च्वासिना दूरवर्ती
संकल्पैस तैर विशति विधिना वैरिणा रुद्धमार्गः ॥९९॥

He, being far away, his path blocked by adverse fate
imagines his body becoming one with yours—
slender with skeletal, paining with burning, tearful
with tear dissolved, deep-sighing with long drawn out sighs. 99

शब्दाख्येयं यदपि किल ते यः सखीनां पुरस्तात
कर्णे लोलः कथयितुम अभूद आननस्पर्शलोभात
सोऽतिक्रान्तः श्रवणविषयं लोचनाभ्याम अदृष्टस
त्वाम उत्कण्ठाविरचितपदं मन्मुखेनेदम आह ||१००||

Who, in presence of your friends
loved to whisper in your ears
what could have been said aloud
longing to touch you, to steal a kiss,
is now far away beyond the reach
of your hearing or eye-sight,
he speaks through me these words,
craving for you in elegant verse. 100

श्यामास्व अङ्गं चकितहरिणीप्रेक्षणे दृष्टिपातं
वक्त्रच्छायां शशिनि शिखिनां बर्हभारेषु केशान
उत्पश्यामि प्रतनुषु नदीवीचिषु भ्रूविलासान
हन्तैकस्मिन क्वचिद अपि न ते चण्डि सादृश्यम अस्ति ॥१०१॥

Your slender limbs—Syama-creepers,
your glance—the doe's tremulous eyes,
your face—the moon,
your luxuriant hair—the peacock's tail,
your eyebrow-play—the brook's ripple.
O fair one! you alone have all these,
there is no one like you in this world. 101

त्वाम आलिख्य प्रणयकुपितां धातुरागै: शिलायाम
आत्मानं ते चरणपतितं यावद इच्चामि कर्तुम
अस्रैस तावन मुहुर उपचितैर दृष्टिर आलुप्यते मे
क्रूरस तस्मिन्न अपि न सहते संगमं नौ कृतान्त: ॥१०२॥

Seized by love's rage I paint you red on the rock
and wish to paint myself prostrating at your feet,
but my eyesight gets blurred by gushing tears,
even here, cruel fate would not allow us to meet. 102

माम आकाशप्रणिहितभुजं निर्दयाश्लेषहेतोर
लब्धायास ते कथम अपि मया स्वप्नसन्दर्शनेषु
पश्यन्तीनां न खलु बहुशो न स्थलीदेवतानां
मुक्तास्थूलास तरुकिसलयेष्व अश्रुलेशाः पतन्ति ॥१०३॥

Seeing my arms outstretched in the air
to embrace you passionately, to kiss you
somehow in my dreams, the tree goddesses will
surely shed tears as big as pearls on tender leaves. 103

भित्त्वा सद्यः किसलयपुटान देवदारुद्रुमाणां
ये तत्क्षीरस्रुतिसुरभयो दक्षिणेन प्रवृत्ताः
आलिङ्ग्यन्ते गुणवति मया ते तुषाराद्रिवाताः
पूर्वं स्पृष्टं यदि किल भवेद अङ्गम एभिस तवेति ॥१०४॥

Sudden Himalayan wind, breaks open
the freshly sprouted pods of the Devadara trees,
blows south fragrant with their sap—
I'll embrace it, my love, thinking
it might have touched your body. 104

Devadara: Himalayan cedar

संक्षिप्यन्ते क्षन इव कथं दीर्घयामा त्रियामा
सर्वावस्थास्व अहर अपि कथं मन्दमन्दातपं स्यात
इत्थं चेतश चटुलनयने दुर्लभप्रार्थनं मे
गाढोष्माभिः कृतम अशरणं त्वद्वियोगव्यथाभिः ॥१०५॥

If only the night with its long hours
could pass in a moment! If only
the hot sun be soft to me at all times!
O doe-eyed, from the bitter pain
of separation from you, my heart has lost
all hope—its desires impossible to attain. 105

नन्व आत्मानं बहु विगणयन्न आत्मनैवावलम्बे
तत्कल्याणि त्वम अपि नितरां मा गमः कातरत्वम
कस्यात्यन्तं सुखम उपनतं दुःखम एकान्ततो वा
नीचौर गच्चत्य उपरि च दशा चक्रनेमिक्रमेण ||१०६||

Reflecting, however, I find strength within,
therefore darling, don't give in
to utter despondency. Who has ever attained
everlasting happiness or suffered endless misery?
The man's condition is like the rim of a wheel
—sometimes up, sometimes down. 106

शापान्तो मे भुजगशयनाद उत्थिते शाङ्र्गपाणौ
शेषान मासान गमय चतुरो लोचने मीलयित्वा
पश्चाद आवां विरहगुणितं तं तम आत्माभिलाषं
निर्वेक्ष्याव: परिणतशरच्चन्द्रिकासु क्षपासु ॥१०७॥

Shut your eyes, the curse will be over
with Vishnu rising from his serpent bed,
these four months will pass by in a jiffy,
then we shall quench our unbridled desires
—intensified by our long separation,
in the full-grown autumn moonlight. 107

भूयश्चाह त्वम अपि शयने कण्ठलग्ना पुरा मे
निद्रां गत्वा किम अपि रुदती सस्वरं विप्रबुद्धा
सान्तर्हासं कथितम असकृत पृच्छतश च त्वया मे
दृष्टः स्वप्ने कितव रमयन काम अपि त्वं मयेति ॥१०८॥

And once again happily we'll be in bed
as before, your arms around my neck,
suddenly, you'll wake up sobbing
and when I would ask the reason,
you'll tell me with half-suppressed laughter
—"You flirt, I saw you in my dream
making love to another woman." 108

एतस्मान मां कुशलिनम अभिज्ञानदानाद् विदित्वा
मा कौलीनाद् असितनयने मय्य अविश्वासिनी भूः
स्नेहान आहुः किम अपि विरहे ध्वंसिनस ते त्व अभोगाद
इष्टे वस्तुन्य उपचितरसाः प्रेमराशीभवन्ति ॥१०९॥

On receiving the message O dusky-eyed,
rest assured I'm well, don't doubt me
believing any scandalous gossip.
They say distance destroys love
ah! on the contrary, in the absence
of pleasure, cravings become stronger,
multiplying into a galaxy of desires. 109

कच्चित सौम्य व्यवसितम इदं बन्धुकृत्यं त्वया मे
प्रत्यादेशान न खलु भवतो धीरतां कल्पयामि
नि:शब्दोऽपि प्रदिशसि जलं याचितश चातकेभ्य:
प्रत्युक्तं हि प्रणयिषु सताम ईप्सितार्थक्रियैव ||११०||

O Cloud, have you decided to do me this favour
as a friend? Your grave look does not mean
your refusal, you offer raindrops in silence
to thirsty Chatakas—for the reply of a noble-soul
to the prayer of the needy is to fulfill his wish. 110

The Chataka bird is believed to drink rain in the air as it falls.

एतत्कृत्वा प्रियमनुचितप्रार्थनावर्तिनो मे
सौहार्दाद्वा विधुर इति वा मय्यनुक्रोशबुद्ध्या।
इष्टान्देशाञ्जलद विचर प्रावृषा संभृतश्रीर्मा
भूदेवं क्षणमपि च ते विद्युता विप्रयोगः ॥१११॥

Having granted my heart's wish
for our friendship's sake or out of pity
O cloud, richly recharged with rain, go
wherever you wish to go. May you never
be separated from the light of your life
like me, even for a moment! 111

ACKNOWLEDGEMENT

I'm grateful to Chaitali Pandya for reading the manuscript carefully and offering me her valuable suggestions.